Who is Angela Peters?

My name is Angela and I was saved in my 30's after many high and low points in my life. Jesus continues to be my one and only source of strength and has inspired me to write this book Reflections of the Heart.

I was born with cerebral palsy a medical condition that makes your muscles contract constantly. Despite my disability and by the grace of God I am able to travel and spread his message of love to people from all walks of life.

I hope my book inspires you to know Jesus Christ in a very personal and real way as I have done.

-Angela

Love the Lord with all your heart, amen.

And we know that all things work together for good to them that love God, to them who are called according to his purpose. -Romans 8:28

Your Love Jesus

Your love Jesus attracts me to remain in your presence.

Your love gives me strength when I have no strength in me.

Your love for me is unconditional.

Jesus your love for me is true.

Lord I can't wait to finally take a walk with you with your hand in mine.

Your love Jesus attracts me to remain by your side and to be faithful to you.

Would You Call Me A Christian?

Would you call me a Christian if you passed by me?
Would you see Christ in me by the way I treated you?
Would Christ's love be poured on you when you were hurting?

I want to be filled with the love of Christ so others will long to have Jesus Christ in their lives.

Jesus Christ loves all mankind. Jesus Christ heals hurting souls. When our Spirit is broken, Jesus Christ makes our spirit whole.

Walking With Jesus

I will walk by my faith knowing you Love me.

Jesus you see the better version of me while some see me different.

It's a dark and scary sometimes In my earthly world!

So hold my hand and carry me until I can walk with you in Heaven.

For we walk by faith, not by sight. -2 Corinthians 5:7

Trust You

Trust you God, I want to trust you for everything.

You think I am beautiful.

I want to trust that you will let someone notice me as long as I notice you first.

I want to trust you for everything today, tomorrow, and every day.

Let me trust you for everything.

The Love of God

The love of God, keeps a smile on my face.
The love of God, fills my soul with joy.
The love that God showed me, tells me God loves me.

God sent his only begotten Son to die on the cross for
you and me. God loves us so much, God gave his only
begotten son, so that we might live.

That's the love of God.

Standing with Me

When I am out in the cold God, You are standing with me.

When the sun is shining and my face is towards the sun, God you are standing with me.

When I am alone God, you are standing with me.

God you are always standing with me.

I can do all things through Christ who strengthens me.
—Philippians 4:13

Sometimes

Sometimes we must be in certain places before we can move forward.

We must walk with God for God to bless our life.

Sometimes we can cry because we regret life choices.

Sometimes we need to remember where we were when we walked away from God.

So we will always let God hold our right hand.

Someday we will see brighter days. God will take us to great places in life, if we always walk in his ways.

Restored

I am restored, I am me again I am happy.
Even though most of my days are dark I am restored.

I am walking in my purpose for my life I am restored.
Back to God's will for my life. God is my all in all, he is
my everything.

When I die God will be all I need.

You see God is all I need now. That's why God is my
everything you see.

Rebuild

God rebuild my life. Rebuild my stolen dreams.

Rebuild my hope for a happy life on earth.
Throw away all my ugly past away.

Rebuild my life all over again. Let me see that I am beautiful.

You don't see my past, you only see my today.
You see all my tomorrow.

So rebuild my life all over again, giving me a brand new life.

Only You

Only you can help me thru the day.
I come to you God, only you can help me.

On you, I rely. Only you can help me.
So I will call on you each and every day.

*You will seek me and find me when you search for me
with all your heart. –Jeremiah 29:13*

May You Find Hope

May you find hope in Jesus when you feel sad.
Smile as the tears run down your face.

God will hold you close as you cry.
Find hope in Jesus today.

When you cry, you will cry tears of joy.
So cry out to God.

Jesus will take your pain and turn it into joy!
So call his name.

He will hear you call to him.
He has open arms, so call on him again.

Lord Waits

There is a place where our Lord waits.
One day he will make his triumphant return.
He will hug his people and he will be our God.
We will be able to look into the eyes of our Redeemer
every single second.
We will be able to sing of his grace.
I can't wait for this beautiful moment.
The moment where I will be able to look into the eyes of
my Savior, never having to walk away from him ever
again.

Live Your Dream

Live your dream.
God put your dream in your heart.
Wait to see your dream come to pass.

In God's timing you will smile.
You will know that you are in God's perfect will for your life.

Delight yourself also in the Lord, and he shall give you the desires of your heart. Psalm 37:4

Jesus is My Sunshine

Jesus is my sunshine on a cloudy day.
When I confess my sins and forsake them he gives me mercy and washes my sins away.
Jesus gives me insight to joust how blessed I really am.
Jesus makes me smile.
That smile allows me to say and sing Jesus is my sunshine.
One day I will hug Jesus so tightly forever.

Have Joy

Joy gives you peace. Have Joy!
Joy makes you smile.
When life brings you down, let the light of Jesus shine through.
Others will see the joy Jesus gives to you!

Jesus is the Head of the Church

Those of us who believe in Jesus and call on him as Lord,
we are the body.

Jesus loves us. Hold us never to let us go
You're perfect people are not.

Jesus helps us to love people.
You alone Jesus can heal a person in every way possible.

The Peace of God

The peace of God gives us hope everlasting.
The peace of God makes us smile when trouble comes
our way.

The peace of God tells us everything will be OK.
The peace of God is in our hearts, safe to stay Forever.

In Your Presence Lord

In Your presence, Lord, all by hurt melts away.

In Your presence, Lord, all my troubles go away.

In Your presence, Lord, all I see is you.

God, you love me so much in your presence, you want to be with me.

In your presence, happy I am.

In your presence I am free from the thoughts that bring me down.

In your presence I see the light.

In your presence you are with me; you listen to praise.

God, you love me. God, you're all I really need.

In your presence I am free!

I Am

God says I am the one who wants to be with you.
I am the one who loves humanity. I am the one who will
never leave your life when you let me in.

I am the one who gave you today.
I want to throw your trash in your life away.
I am the one who knows you, so seek me when you are
ready

I may not give you everything you want but I will give
you everything you need.

When you die you will be with me Jesus.
I am the one who gives you eternal life totally free

How Much You Mean to Me

When I say I love you Lord do you see how much I mean it? Since you loved me first before I even knew your name, did you smile down upon me since you already knew the very call upon my life?

Keep your hand in mine as we run the ministry together. Even though I am young, let me be focused on the very calling.

You called me to so people can come to the very knowledge of you.

I'm Glad

I am glad you are in my life.
I'm glad that God gave us friends that
We can love and be loved by.

You add sunshine to my day by putting a
Smile on my face.

A friend loves at all times, and a brother is born for adversity. –Proverbs 17:17

Heaven

I wish I could reach heaven tonight.
In heaven I will be held so tight like never before in all my life.

Running to Jesus on both feet I wish I could reach heaven tonight. I wish I could reach heaven on all my boring days of my life.

Sooner than later the sky will open up and, all who believe In Jesus will leave this lonely place called earth going to heaven.

God Take me by the Hand

God take me by the right hand.
Lead me on the right path.
Dance with me in the sun!
Keep me on the right path walking with you.
Jesus is the best thing I can ever do.

*For I, the LORD your God, hold your right hand; it is I who
say to you, "Fear not, I am the one who helps you."*
–Isaiah 41:13

Happy

To be happy, let me reach out to people so I can be happy.

Let me get my mind off me God, for you will take care of my every need.

Free me from myself. I lay myself down, let me happy in every way.

With everything, may I be willing to give myself to you, God.

You know everything I need, when I need it.

We Tell God to Bless America

We tell God to bless America by the stickers we own that
say, "God Bless America!" Yet we, as a nation, do not
seek God as we once did.

We tell God to bless America,
Yet we remove God from our schools. We tell God to
bless America, yet seats are empty on Sunday in
churches.
We tell God to bless America, yet we do not welcome
God in our society. We live our lives without God in our
nation, yet we tell God to bless America.

"How long can God bless a nation where God is not
welcomed? "

God Believe

God Believe in me when I don't believe in myself.
Let me believe that you will take me to great places in my life.

Never being in the same place I want to believe that you have the very best plan for my life.

Jesus said to him, "Because you have seen me, have you believed? Blessed are they who did not see, and yet believed." -John 20:29

Glad

When I woke up to face the sun; let me be glad in that day. Let me be glad that you let me live another day.

Let me make every day count. Every day comes from you God. Days, filled with purpose, you give to me until Jesus comes to get me, or I draw my last breath.

Let me be glad in every day. God, you planted me where you wanted me to be.

As I Pray

As I pray God, you hear every word.
As I pray, when my heart is heavy, God you see every
tear that falls from my eyes.

As I pray, my prayers are sent up to heaven. God
answers prayers the way he wants to. I have seen
answered prayers in my life, over and over again.

So, as I pray, God hears my prayers. God hears your
prayers too.

The prayer of a righteous man is powerful and effective.
–James 5:16

A New Day

A new day will come to change yesterday. Yesterday will become tomorrow.

Tomorrow live one day at a time. Tomorrow you will never know what will come to be.

Love

Love is blind.
Love keeps fighting to stay together as one.
True love knows no end. True love fights to the very end.

A Coat to Wear

God gave us a coat to wear in life. A purpose was given for our lives.

The coat you wear in life may be heavy at times. Cast your cares upon the Lord.

The Lord will walk with us as we do what we are called to do.

When you get your coat in life, that coat will be special. The coat was only meant for you to wear.

We all have a purpose in life. So stand strong in the Lord, as you do what the Lord has called you to do.

God Is Love

God will never leave me and forsake me. As I am
stripped from everything the world would call fun.

God is opening doors for me right and left in order for
me to see his faithfulness. God will always be the honey
from the rock who will always satisfy me.

God is love. God's love will never go away from me.

*But he would feed you with the finest of the wheat, and
with honey from the rock I would satisfy you.*
– Psalm 81:16

Notes

Notes

Notes

Notes

Made in the USA
Columbia, SC
10 November 2020